ISLANDIA

VOLUME 1

BOREAL LANDING

Script and artwork: Marc Védrines

Colours: Lætitia Schwendimann

CINEBOOK
The 9th Art Publisher

Original title: Islandia 1 – Escale boréale

Translator: Mark Bence
Editor: Erica Olson Jeffrey
Lettering and text layout: Design Amorandi
Printed in Spain by EGEDSA
This edition first published in Great Britain in 2019 by
Cinebook Ltd
56 Beech Avenue
Canterbury, Kent
CT4 7TA
www.cinebook.com
A CIP catalogue record for this book
is available from the British Library
ISBN 978-1-84918-434-2

CINEBOOK
The 9th Art Publisher

EVERYTHING PACKED?
YES, I EVEN PUT IN ANOTHER WARM VEST FOR YOU.
YOU DON'T SEEM VERY SAD THAT I'M LEAVING TODAY...
YOU KNOW, IT'S LIKE A RITUAL. I'M USED TO STAYING ALONE WITH THE CHILDREN.
YOU MIGHT BE USED TO IT, BUT YOU LOOK ALMOST HAPPY...
WHAT'S GOT INTO YOU?
NOTHING... I JUST WONDER WHAT YOU DO WHEN I'M AWAY.
YOU KNOW WHAT I DO ON THAT WRETCHED BOAT. YOU'RE EITHER ONBOARD OR OVERBOARD!
DON'T BE SILLY!
YOU KNOW WE'VE GOT NO CHOICE... FISHING'S WHAT PAYS BEST. BUT P'RAPS WE'LL GET RICH ONE DAY, WHO KNOWS?
YOU SOUND LIKE YOUR MOTHER... ACH, YOUR FAMILY... AND WHAT ABOUT JACQUES?! I OUGHT TO TAKE HIM ALONG; WE'D EARN EVEN MORE. YOU CAN'T CODDLE HIM FOR EVER.
I PROMISED MY SISTER THAT HE'D HAVE A BETTER LIFE THAN US...
JUST LIKE I SAID: YOU COULDN'T CARE LESS ABOUT ME... AND YOU'LL MAKE THE BOY INTO A LAZYBONES.
HE TURNS SIXTEEN THIS YEAR. AT HIS AGE, I'D BEEN AT WORK FOR FIVE YEARS ALREADY! REMEMBER HE'S ANOTHER MOUTH TO FEED, AND I DON—
JACQUES?
HOW LONG HAVE YOU BEEN STANDING THERE?

I WANTED TO WATCH THE SHIPS LEAVING...
I WANNA GO TOO! I DON'T WANNA BE ON MY OWN...
WELL, LET'S ALL GO TOGETHER, THEN, SINCE WE'RE UP...
IF IT MEANS THAT MUCH TO YOU...
I'M SORRY ABOUT EARLIER... I...
I'M SICK OF LEAVING FOR MONTHS... THIS IS MY LAST FISHING SEASON.
LET GO O' ME!
THE MARSHALS!
YOU KEEP QUIET!
ALL RIGHT, I KNOW THE WAY!

WE WERE JUST WAITING FOR YOU, SEAMAN...
THANK YOU, GENTLEMEN.
TAKE HIM AWAY!

ETERNAL LORD GOD, WHO ALONE SPREADS OUT THE HEAVENS AND RULES THE RAGING OF THE SEA, VOUCHSAFE TO TAKE OUR HUMBLE SELVES INTO THY ALMIGHTY AND MOST GRACIOUS PROTECTION...
PRESERVE US FROM THE DANGERS OF THE SEA. BE MERCIFUL, THAT WE MAY RETURN HOME TO ENJOY THE BLESSINGS OF THE FRUITS OF OUR LABOUR IN THANKFUL RECOLLECTION OF THY INFINITE BOUNTY...
LET US PRAISE AND GLORIFY JESUS CHRIST, OUR LORD... AMEN...
AMEN...
A DROP OF BRANDY ALL ROUND, TO CELEBRATE OUR DEPARTURE.
CLAP
HURRAY!
JUST LOOK WHAT I'VE FOUND...
SHIP'S RATS AIN'T WHAT THEY USED TO BE!
THERE'S A YOUNG STOWAWAY ABOARD, CAPTAIN. NO ONE SEEMS TO KNOW WHAT HE WANTS.
HMM, HE CERTAINLY HAS STYLE...
THIS IS INTOLERABLE, CAPTAIN! WE MUST MAKE AN EXAMPLE OF HIM. WE CAN'T TURN BACK NOW.
INDEED. LOCK HIM IN THE HOLD FOR A DAY, AS A LESSON; THEN WE'LL PUT HIM TO WORK. THAT SHOULD BRING HIM TO HIS SENSES.
YOU COULD'VE BEEN THROWN OVERBOARD! YOU'RE IN LUCK; WE'LL KEEP YOU IN THE DARK FOR A WEEK ON DRY BREAD AND WATER!

HEY, YOU!
WHAT THE HELL ARE YOU DOIN' DOWN HERE?
THIS AIN'T NO PLACE FOR YOUNG'UNS!

DID I SCARE YOU?
STAY SITTIN' DOWN. YOU CAN'T GO VERY FAR, ANYHOW.
GOT PUNISHED TOO, EH? IT'S NO JOKE UP THERE. TIME'LL PASS FASTER NOW THERE'S TWO OF US...
LEMME SEE WHAT YOU'RE SCRIBBLIN'!
WHAT'S ALL THIS? SKETCHES? THOUGHT YOU'D BE WRITIN' TO YOUR MOTHER...
I'M NO EXPERT, BUT IT DON'T LOOK PRETTY.
HERE!
DOODLIN' WEIRD STUFF... YOU'RE AN ODD ONE FOR YOUR AGE. QUIET AS A MOUSE, TOO.
DON'T BE SHY! LEMME SEE YOUR MITTS!
HMM, THESE HANDS'VE NEVER DONE A DAY'S WORK!
THIS AIN'T MY FIRST ROMANCE WITH THE BRINY, SEE! I EVEN LEFT HER A SOUVENIR! WHAT WITH THE WIND, FREEZIN' WATER AND SALT, THE TINIEST SCRATCH ROTS IMMEDIATELY.
FISHIN' THE GRAND BANKS IS NO TRADE FOR SISSIES. YOU'LL HAVE IT HARD, GIVEN YOUR SIZE. THOUGHT YOU WAS A LASS, TO START WITH! HMPH, P'RAPS THEY'LL JUST GET YOU SCRUBBIN' THE DECKS.
THERE'S A SIX- TO EIGHT-POUND LEAD WEIGHT ON THE LINE WE HAUL UP AND DOWN ALL DAY LONG. A CATCH O' COD CAN WEIGH FORTY POUNDS. STRAINS YOUR BONES, IT DOES! THE SEA'S A CRUEL MISTRESS...
I DIDN'T WANNA SERVE ON THIS GALLEY AGAIN, BUT THE CAP'N SWEET-TALKED ME IN THE TAVERN. FLASHED MONEY AROUND, HANDED ME SOME UP FRONT... BEFORE I KNEW IT, I WAS BACK IN THE SHIT...
ONCE I SOBERED UP AND REALISED WHAT I'D DONE, I RAN FOR IT, BUT THE BASTARDS CAUGHT ME. DON'T THINK I'M WORK-SHY, MIND YOU. WE ALL TRY TO GET BY...
NOTHING IN THIS LIFE COMES FREE...
JACQUES!
JACQUES!
UNCLE? IS THAT YOU?

YEAH... IT'S ME...
SHHH... KEEP YOUR VOICE DOWN...
WHY ARE YOU HERE? I'LL GET IN SERIOUS TROUBLE FOR YOUR ANTICS! AND DON'T GO TELLING ANYONE WE'RE RELATED, YOU HEAR?!
I WON'T... I WANTED TO TRAVEL... ER, I MEAN, LEARN HOW TO FISH...
SO, YOU FINALLY DECIDED TO BE A MAN AND MAKE YOURSELF USEFUL!
HERE'S A FEW BISCUITS FOR YOU...
I HAVE TO GO. WE'RE PLAYING DICE TO PICK OUR FISHING POSITIONS.
THANKS.
FLUKY BEGGAR!
TREBLE SIX! I'VE THRASHED YOU!
I'LL FISH FROM THE FORECASTLE!
THAT DIDN'T COUNT! ONE OF THE DICE HIT HIS HAND!
YOU'VE GOT THE LUCK OF THE DEVIL!
IT BOUNCED. T'AIN'T FAIR!
NAH, NAH... ROLL 'EM AGAIN.
ALL RIGHT, BUT I'M ONLY ROLLIN' ONE!
HE SHOULD'VE MOVED HIS HAND!
THAT'S PLAIN CHEATIN'...
YOU AIN'T GOT THE BALLS TO ROLL 'EM AGAIN!
FORGET THE DICE... I'M GOIN' FOR YOUR TEETH!

NEVER SEEN THE LIKE IN TEN YEARS AT SEA...
YEAH, THIS FIRST MATE'S A REAL SLAVE DRIVER! LET'S TALK TO THE CAP'N. HE NEVER TREATS US THAT WAY.
DON'T RECKON THERE'S MUCH WE CAN DO. THEY SAY THE MATE'S THE OWNER'S SON. THE CAP'N HAS TO TAKE IT LIKE THE REST OF US...
JUST WHAT WE NEED, A DADDY'S BOY!
DON'T GIMME THAT RUBBISH! THIS CAN'T GO ON! SOON WON'T BE ENOUGH OF US LEFT TO MAN THE SHIP!
WELCOME TO THE FRESH AIR, SHIPMATES!
CAPTAIN! THE CREW HAVE DEFIED ORDERS AND FREED THE MEN I ARRESTED!
SINCE WE CAN'T LOCK EVERYONE UP, I SUGGEST THEY BE GIVEN THE LASH!
I HAD THEM RELEASED... WE'RE NOT UNDER MILITARY COMMAND; THIS IS A MERCHANT SHIP. OFFICERS SHOULDN'T INSPIRE MORE FEAR THAN THE ENEMY.
BUT THOSE MEN DESERVE TO BE—
POSSIBLY, BUT WORRY NOT; THE TOIL THAT AWAITS THEM OFF THE ICELANDIC COAST WILL SOON PACIFY THEM... AND NOTHING LIKE A TOT OF RUM TO GET THEM EATING OUT OF YOUR HAND.
THEY DON'T TEACH SUCH THINGS AT THE NAVAL SCHOOL YOU LEFT SO RECENTLY... TRUST MY EXPERIENCE. THIS ISN'T MY FIRST VOYAGE, YOU KNOW...
WHAT ARE YOU INSINUATING?
DON'T FORGET WHAT YOU OWE MY FAMILY! NOT EVERY PORT CAN BOAST A VESSEL LIKE THIS!
YOUR FATHER PLACED ME IN COMMAND OF THE SHIP. I'M ONLY RESPONSIBLE TO HIM, AND FOR THE AMOUNT OF FISH WE BRING BACK...

WHAT A PEDANTIC YOUNG FOOL.
HE WAS FORCED UPON ME, LIEUTENANT. WE SHALL HAVE TO MANAGE...
YOU WERE RIGHT TO SHOW HIM WHO'S MASTER ON BOARD.
DON'T WORRY, THERE'S ONLY ONE, AND IT IS I!
I'M IN FULL CONTRO—
CAPTAIN!
CAPTAIN?
CAPTAIN? SIR?
NONE OF US ARE HERE BY CHOICE, JACQUES!
IT MAKES NO SENSE!
WHY DID YOU COME?
I WANTED TO LEARN HOW TO FISH...
YOU'RE HAVING ME ON! WHY ARE YOU HERE?
I WANT TO BE A FISHERMAN, LIKE YOU!
D'YOU TAKE ME FOR A FOOL?! WHY THE HELL ARE YOU HERE?!
ICELAND... I WANT TO GO TO ICELAND...
TO ICELAND?
HAA HAAA HAAA! YOU'RE ON THE WRONG BOAT, THEN! WE DON'T STOP THERE! HAAA HAA HAAA HA!
WHAT DO YOU WANT ON THAT DEVIL'S ISLAND, ANYWAY?

I FEAR YOUR ANKLE MAY BE BROKEN. YOU MUST TRY NOT TO MOVE IT. I CAN EASE THE PAIN, BUT IT WILL TAKE A WHILE TO HEAL.
ENOUGH OF YOUR BABBLING! GIVE ME SOMETHING... ANYTHING! I HAVE TO BE ON MY FEET AS SOON AS POSSIBLE. I CAN'T LEAVE THAT WEASEL IN CHARGE!
FOR THAT, YOU'LL REQUIRE A SAINT. I'M NOT A MIRACLE WORKER!
IT'S LIKE A GAME OF CHESS HERE. THERE'S THE KING, QUEEN, AND IMPORTANT PIECES, THEN THE PAWNS NO ONE GIVES A DAMN ABOUT. IT'S A POWER STRUGGLE AND YOU'RE A PAWN. THERE'S A FEW RULES TO STOP YOU ENDING UP ON THE WRONG SQUARE.
FOLLOW ME!
IT'S ALL LAID OUT. WE OBEY OFFICERS, BUT AMONG US, IT'S EVERY MAN FOR HIMSELF. TO FISH, WE SLIP INTO A BARREL TO PROTECT US FROM THE COLD, SPRAY, AND WIND. THERE'S ONE EACH, AND WE STAY IN THE SAME PLACES TILL THE END. EVERY COD WE CATCH, WE CUT OUT ITS TONGUE AND PUT IT IN A BASKET FOR THE COUNT. STOPS ANY CHEATING.
WHERE DO I STAND?
ALL THE POSTS ARE TAKEN... YOU'VE NEVER EVEN CRACKED OPEN AN OYSTER; THEY'LL PROBABLY PUT YOU ON SLICING DUTY. YOU CHOP OFF THE FISH HEADS, TOSS THEM ASIDE FOR US TO EAT, THEN GUT THE REST... IF YOU FIND WORMS, KEEP THEM FOR BAIT. OH, AND DON'T THROW AWAY THE LIVER; IT'S USED TO MAKE OIL... CLEAR?
DON'T LOOK SO DISGUSTED... DID YOU GET ALL THAT?
YES, UNCLE...
DON'T CALL ME THAT HERE! HOW MANY MORE TIMES?!
UNCLE!!!

DON'T WORRY YER HEAD, LAD! IT WAS ONLY AN ACCIDENT...
ACCIDENT? NEVER SEEN A HALYARD SNAP LIKE THAT! IT'S A SIGN THAT GOD WANTED TO CALL HIM HOME, I TELL YA!
LOSIN' THREE LI'L TEETH AIN'T GONNA SEND HIM TO HEAVEN... HE'LL PULL THROUGH!
MAYBE, BUT IT MUST BE A SIGN O' DIVINE PUNISHMENT. I SAW HIM WALLOP THE LAD.
IF THAT'S WHY GOD PUNISHED HIM, WE'D ALL BE DEAD! SIT YOUR ARSE DOWN WITH US, KID...
AND TREAT HIM WITH RESPECT OR ... WATCH OUT!
HA HA HA HA HA HA HA
HERE, BOY, YOU'VE EARNED THE RIGHT TO SIP A DRAM WITH US! YOU'LL SEE THE WORLD NOW YOU'RE A REAL SAILOR...
WILL WE BE STOPPING OFF IN ICELAND?
ICELAND? NO TIME. FISHING'S NOT A PLEASURE CRUISE! WE'D ONLY LAND THERE IF WE WERE DAMAGED...
WE'RE CLOSE ENOUGH TO THAT DISMAL LAND AS IT IS. THEY OUGHT TO DEPORT CONVICTS THERE. IT'S THE GATES OF HELL!
THIS HERE IS HELL! STUCK WITH THE SAME FELLAS FOR MONTHS, ALL UNDERPAID, AND D'YOU THINK THIS LAD'S HERE BY CHANCE?
NOTHING STUPID OR RECKLESS ABOUT HIM. THAT THERE IDIOT'S HIS UNCLE, OR SO HE SAID...
IS IT TRUE? WHAT ARE YOU HIDING?
NOTHING! I...
SO, IS THAT BEGGAR YER FAMILY?
YOU HERE TO SPY ON US?
HE MADE ME COME. MY MOTHER DIED, SO I LIVE WITH MY AUNT. UNCLE WANTED ME TO EARN MY KEEP, AND THAT'S WHY I'M HERE...
SOMETHIN' FISHY 'BOUT HIS STORY...
SAID I HAD A BAD FEELIN' ABOUT THE KID...
YOU'D BETTER GO. ACT LIKE YOU'RE TIRED. THERE'S A SPARE PLACE IN MY BUNK, IF YOU WANT...

IT'S ME. LIGHTS OUT. EVERYONE IN BED...
SHOVE OVER SO WE CAN SNUGGLE UP WARM... SHUSH... DON'T BE AFRAID...
SHHH...
BUT...
NOT SO FAST, MY PRETTY...
HANDS OFF, OR YOU'LL GET A REAL CLOSE SHAVE!
UNDERSTAND THIS: ANYTHING GOES DOWN THERE! IF I WAS YOU, I'D SLEEP SOMEWHERE ELSE. THE WEAKEST GET TAKEN...
ROOK TAKES PAWN!
WHAT?
A REAL SAILOR'S MOST FAITHFUL COMPANION IS A GOOD BLADE. GUARANTEES YOUR LIFE. UNBEATABLE FOR GETTING OUT OF ANY SITUATION.
AND IF YOU FALL INTO THE SEA?
......
WHAT'S WRONG?
GRRR
GNAAA

NOO NOOOAAAAAAAAAAAARRRRGGHH...
BLOODY HELL!
MOVE YOUR ARSES! HELP ME GET HIM DOWN! P'RAPS HE'S STILL ALIVE!
CAN YOU HEAR ME?
WHAT HAPPENED?
HE'S STILL BREATHING!
I... I... I DUNNO HOW I ... GOT TANGLED UP... THE ROPES SNAKED ROUND ME LIKE THEY WAS ALIVE, I SWEAR ON MY LIFE... I AIN'T MAD... JUST BEFORE, I HAD A FLASH... A VOICE IN MY HEAD...
...WHISPERING: 'GET RID OF THAT ONE!'

IS IT TOO MUCH TO ASK TO BE GIVEN SOME DECENT FOOD?
WHAT WERE YOU EXPECTING?
WE CARRY MINIMUM RATIONS. ALL ROOM IN THE HOLD IS FOR THE FISH!
...AND BRANDY FOR THOSE DRUNKARDS YOU CALL YOUR CREW...
MOREOVER, IN THE EXQUISITE ATLANTIC, FRESH FOOD WOULD SEEM TO BE IN ABUNDANCE...
ONCE THE FISHING BEGINS, YOU'LL EAT FISH, DAY IN, DAY OUT...
BY THE TIME WE RETURN, EVEN THE SMELL WILL REVOLT YOU, SO DON'T COMPLAIN, AND EAT WHAT'S ON YOUR PLATE!
AFTER THREE WEEKS AT SEA, WE SHOULD BE FISHING ALREADY, IF I'M NOT MISTAKEN! AT LEAST THAT'S WHAT YOU PROMISED MY FATHER...
LOCKED AWAY IN YOUR QUARTERS, DO YOU EVEN HAVE THE SLIGHTEST IDEA WHERE WE ARE? ADMIT IT, YOU'RE LOST!
THE NAVAL SCHOOL FROM WHICH YOU HAVE JUST GRADUATED MUST HAVE NEGLECTED TO MENTION THAT, SINCE WE'VE PASSED THE FAEROE ISLANDS, OUR COMPASS IS UNUSABLE. AT THIS LATITUDE, ITS NEEDLE DEVIATES BY AT LEAST 25 DEGREES AND SOLAR NAVIGATION IS IMPOSSIBLE, SO WE RELY PURELY ON MARITIME EXPERIENCE. TRUST ME, WE MUST BE FAIRLY CLOSE.
THANK THE LORD! THE MEN ARE WOEFULLY INACTIVE. SPECULATION AND GOSSIP ARE RIFE...
I WHOLEHEARTEDLY AGREE, LIEUTENANT!
WHAT DO YOU MEAN? EXPLAIN!
RUMOUR HAS IT THAT THE BOY IS A JINX. THE MEN TELL STORIES THAT SEEM TO PROVE IT, AND YOU'VE BEEN ABSENT FOR SEVERAL WEEKS. SEEING YOU WOULD REASSURE THEM...
IF WE HAVE TO THROW THE BOY TO THE SHARKS TO CALM THEM, SO BE IT...
IT'S NOTHING BUT OLD WIVES' TALES...
KNOCK
KNOCK
YES, COME IN!
CAP'N, SIR! THEY'RE SAYIN' ICELAND'S IN SIGHT!

THE LINES ARE CAST AND THE MEN ARE AT THEIR POSTS, CAPTAIN.
SPLENDID!
AH, ICELAND! SMELL THAT AIR – PURE AS THE FIRST DAYS OF CREATION!
TO ALL WHO APPROACH HER, THIS LAND IS AS COQUETTISH AS A FINE LADY. FREQUENTLY VEILED LIKE AN ORIENTAL BRIDE, SHE REVEALS HERSELF TO HOPEFUL ADMIRERS IN A VARIETY OF WAYS, ON A WHIM.
THE FISHING LOOKS PROMISING. I WONDER WHY THE COD BITE BETTER AT NIGHT...
PERHAPS THEY TOO HAVE WHIMS? LIKE A MODEST WOMAN WHO WILL ONLY SUBMIT IN THE DARK.
I WAS UNAWARE OF YOUR POETIC TALENT, LIEUTENANT.
AS WAS I!
IN ANY CASE, EVERYTHING SEEMS IN ORDER AGAIN. WORK IS UNDERWAY... BUT WHAT'S BECOME OF THE BOY? IS HE HIDING?
HE RETREATED TO THE MAIN-TOPMAST TWO DAYS AGO...
WHAT?
WE CAN'T GET HIM DOWN. HE'S SET HIMSELF UP, USING ITEMS THAT HE STOLE...
HE'S LOST HIS MIND! WE SIMPLY MUST DO SOMETHING!

COME DOWN, LAD! FEAR NOT! WE PROMISE NOT TO HURT YOU!
DOESN'T SEEM TO BE MOVING...
YOU CAN'T REASON WITH THIS DEMON LIKE THAT. WE'LL HAVE TO GET HIM BY FORCE!
HE'LL COME DOWN EVENTUALLY.
SO FAR, HE'S BEEN FENDING FOR HIMSELF...
BONK
WHAT IS IT? A MESSAGE?
'DROP ME OFF IN ICELAND AND YOU'LL HEAR THE LAST OF ME...'
HE CAN WRITE? HOW SURPRISING!
HE CERTAINLY IS RESOURCEFUL, BUT I DON'T QUITE SEE WHAT HE'S AFTER. WE CAN'T ACCEDE TO HIS DEMAND ANYWAY. LANDING IN ICELAND IS FRAUGHT WITH DANGER.
WE MUST ACT! THIS HAS GONE ON TOO LONG!
DID YOU NOTICE THESE ODD SQUIGGLES OR SYMBOLS?
ANY IDEA WHAT IT COULD MEAN?
NO!
THUD
WHAT IS IT?
ALL IT SAYS IS: 'WELL?'
WELL, WE'LL REWARD HIS IMPATIENCE!
DON'T TELL ME HE JUST EMPTIED HIS CHAMBER POT ON US!
I CAN'T GET TO HIM! HE'S GOT SOME KIND OF LANCE!
YOU'LL REGRET THAT, YOU BRAT!
DON'T SAY A WORD, SAILOR!

THE PLAN IS SIMPLE. LISTEN CAREFULLY.
WE STRETCH ROPES HERE AND HERE TO REACH HIM FROM THE MIZZEN MAST AND FOREMAST.
IS THAT CLEAR ENOUGH?
CAPTAIN! HE'S JUST DROPPED A NEW MESSAGE!
URGENT MEETING! ALL HANDS ON DECK IMMEDIATELY!

WE MUST ACT QUICKLY! THE MUTINEER IS NOW THREATENING TO HURL BURNING EMBERS DOWN FROM HIS ROOST AND SET THE SHIP ON FIRE, UNLESS WE AGREE TO HIS TERMS AND LEAVE HIM IN ICELAND!
WE'LL SHOW HIM THE PRICE OF DEFYING AUTHORITY! WE'LL BEGI—
BOOOM
THE DANES! ALL HANDS TO YOUR STATIONS! SET SAIL!!!
WE OUGHT TO COMPLY WITH THEIR WARNING SHOTS. WE'RE NO MATCH FOR A WARSHIP. YOU'RE FORGETTING MY FATHER'S ADVICE...
OF COURSE WE WON'T ENGAGE THEM IN COMBAT, BUT WE'RE LIGHTER AND FASTER. WE CAN OUTRUN THEM.
KABLAM

BOOOOM
CRACK
BRRRROOOOOOOOOOmmm–
CAPTAIN! WE'RE BREAKING AWAY BUT APPROACHING THE COAST. IT'S DANGEROUS IN THIS FOG!
NO, IT'S PERFECT! THIS FOG IS OUR CHANCE! FULL SPEED AHEAD!
CAN'T SEE A THING! LORD GOD, DO NOT FORSAKE US! HELP US ESCAPE THE DAMN DANES…
HEY, WHAT…
JACQUES, STOP!!!

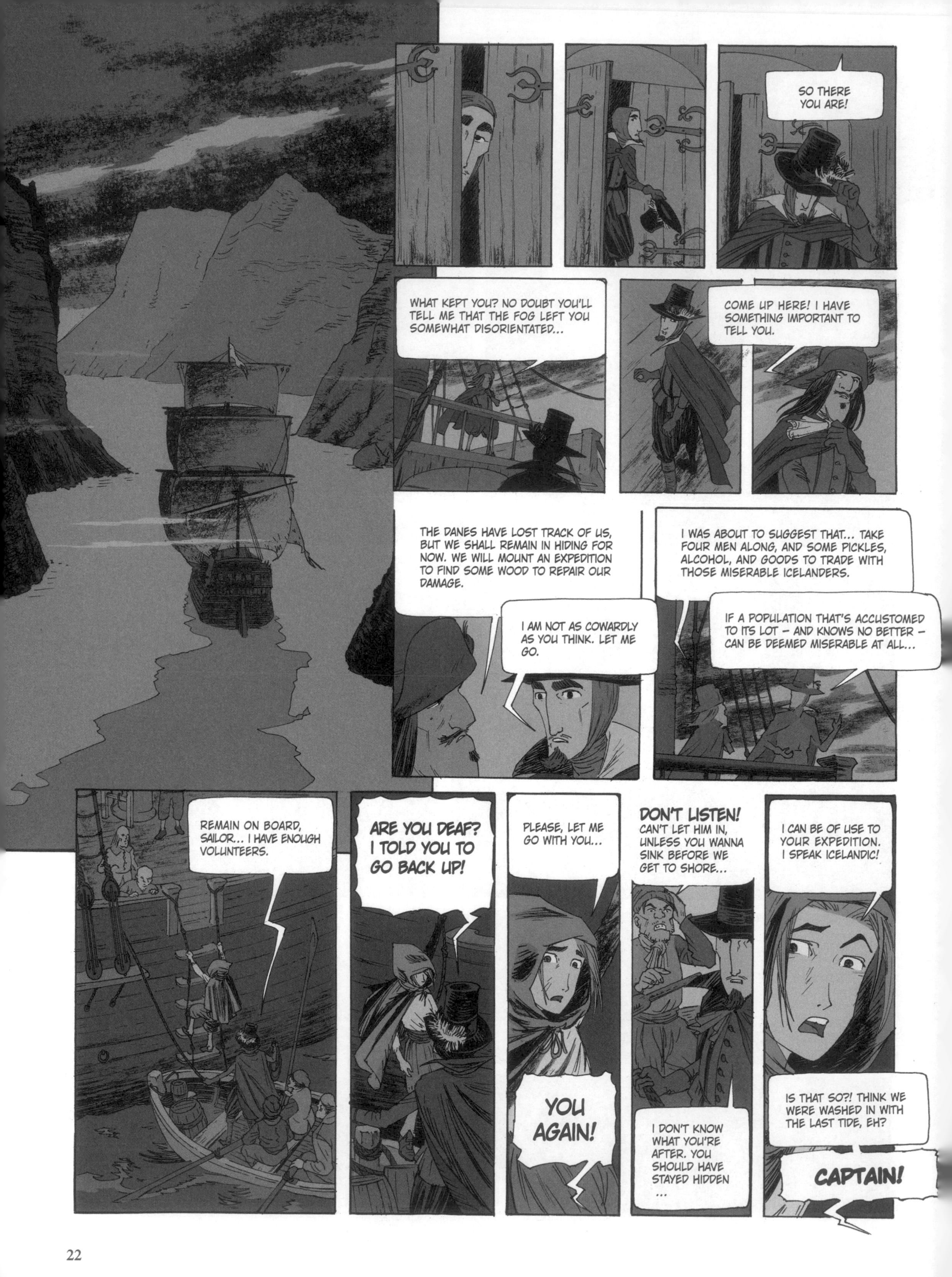

22

BUT I COULD'VE HELPED! I DO SPEAK ICELANDIC! ÉG TALA ÍSLENSKU!
FÁVITINN ÞINN!
YOUR PLACE IS DOWN IN THE HOLD! TAKE HIM AWAY!
DAMN HIM. I'M STARTING TO BELIEVE THE RUMOURS. IF HE'S FROM HELL, SEND HIM BACK!
CAPTAIN, LOOK HERE!
CONTACTS WITH THE LOCALS DON'T SEEM TO BE GOING TOO WELL...
PASS ME THE SPYGLASS!
UNBELIEVABLE! HE CAN'T BE TRUSTED WITH ANYTHING...
A BAD DIPLOMAT AS WELL AS A BAD SAILOR!
WHAT ARE THEY DOING? THEY'RE GETTING BACK IN THE BOAT!
WHAT ARE YOU PLAYING AT?
LOOK WHAT I FOUND! IT'S FROM THE MARIE-JEANNE!
THERE'S PLENTY MORE. I EVEN SAW THE SHIP'S BELL. PROVIDENCE LED US HERE!
MY FATHER HAD NO NEWS OF HIS SHIP OR HER CREW FOR FOUR YEARS. WE NEED TO INVESTIGATE. THE ICELANDERS MUST KNOW SOMETHING. PERHAPS THEY EVEN RANSACKED HER!
I NEED THAT BOY, IF HE REALLY SPEAKS THE LANGUAGE.
DON'T WORRY: I'LL HAVE MY EYE ON HIM...

I'M COLD!
LIKE THAT, I KNOW YOU WON'T GO FAR. YOU WANTED TO COME? HERE YOU ARE.
NOW KEEP UP WITH ME!
DO AS I TELL YOU! NO TRICKERY, OR I'LL—
PETTA ER ALLT OG SUMT SEM ÉG VEIT.
SO? TRANSLATE! WHAT'S HIS EXPLANATION?
HE SAYS IT'S NOT HIS FAULT... THE SHIP MUST HAVE CAPSIZED OFF THE COAST. THE SEA WASHED UP THOSE OBJECTS HE FOUND...
AS FOR THE CREW, HE ONLY SAW THE BODIES SWEPT ASHORE BY THE WAVES. THEY ALL HAD A CHRISTIAN BURIAL.
HE ALSO SAYS THAT I'M UNDERDRESSED FOR FEBRUARY ...
A LITTLE EXERCISE IS GOOD FOR KEEPING WARM!
ASK HIM WHERE THEY'RE BURIED. I WANT TO SEE... YOU'LL COME ALONG AS MY GUIDE.
'IT'S VERY SIMPLE: WALK BACK UP THE FJORD, THROUGH THE FOREST, THEN MAKE FOR THE HILL OPPOSITE...'
HOW MUCH FURTHER?
THE NEXT HILL AFTER THE FOREST.
I SEE NO FOREST. HE'S TAKEN US FOR A RIDE!
YOU'RE IN AN ICELANDIC FOREST RIGHT NOW!
'WHEN YOU SEE A VARÐA, YOU'LL BE CLOSE. PASS TO THE RIGHT OF IT AND GO UPHILL.'
THIS IS THE MARKER. NOT FAR NOW.

THERE IT IS. WE HAVE TO PASS TO THE LEFT TO REACH IT...
CAWW CAWW
OH YES, I SEE SOME CROSSES.
LET'S GO.
SHLOOFF
?
.....
GET BACK, NOW!
HURRY!
I'M TRYING!
LOOK! HE'S RUNNING!
'MAKE SURE YOU KEEP TO THE RIGHT! IT'S MARSHY THERE, WITH QUICKSAND HIDDEN UNDERNEATH THE SNOW!'
LITTLE SWINE!
.....
JACQUES?
THIS SORT OF EXERCISE WON'T KEEP YOU WARM!
AND ME!
DON'T LEAVE ME!
HE'S OFF AGAIN, LIKE A RABBIT! HE WON'T GET FAR, DRESSED LIKE THAT ...

EVENING, MAGNÚS. WONDERS WILL NEVER CEASE. IS BUSINESS PICKING UP?
HELLO, JÓN. YES, IT'S A MIRACLE.
BRANDY, PICKLES, AND ROPES FOR SOME OLD DRIFTWOOD... THOSE FRENCHMEN WERE HEAVEN-SENT!
OUR ONCE-GLORIOUS PEOPLE FROM THE TIME OF THE SAGAS ARE NOW COMPELLED TO SURVIVE AT THE MERCY OF GOD AND THE DANISH KING... THEIR TRADE MONOPOLY DRIVES US DEEPER INTO MISERY BY THE DAY.
ANYHOW, I HOPE YOU'LL KEEP IT QUIET. WE MERCHANTS MUSTN'T BREAK THE LAW. YOU KNOW WHAT I FACE...
FOLKS HAVE BEEN FLOGGED TO DEATH FOR LESS!
YOU KNOW ME ... AND HOW MUCH I LOATHE THE COLONISERS. BE THEY DAMNED. AND THEIR KING!
OUR LORD GOD IS MIGHTIER THAN THE KING!
SÉRA* GUÐMUNDUR!
*COMMON WORD FOR A PASTOR
HE HATH WILLED THAT THERE BE POOR FOLK SO THE RICH MAY LEARN FROM THEM.
BUT, FATHER, THE HOLY SCRIPTURES SAY THAT OUR LORD LEFT MAN TO JUDGE RIGHT FROM WRONG. IT'S NOT HIS WILL TO SELL THE ICELANDERS ROTTING GOODS AND TAKE THEIR WEALTH; IT'S THE WILL OF THE DANES!
ALAS, WE ARE BUT SINNERS WHO BRING ALL GOOD OR ILL UPON OURSELVES. IN THE PAST, THE ICELANDIC PEOPLE LIVED IN IGNORANCE...
NOW THEY MUST DO PENANCE.
THEN, LET US PRAY FOR DIVINE JUSTICE TO REIGN OVER THE DANES, TOO!
WHAT BRINGS YOU HERE, SÉRA GUÐMUNDUR? SUCH A JOURNEY!
I'VE COME FOR MEDICINE. VIGFÚS'S WIFE IS GRAVELY ILL AT SNOTRUNES FARM. I MUST HASTEN, OR SHE WILL REQUIRE THE LAST RITES.
COME. I THINK I HAVE WHAT YOU NEED.

THANKS. GOD BLESS YOU!
GOODBYE AND TAKE CARE. THE SKIES ARE CLOUDING OVER.
SUCH A MAN OF FAITH. I HOPE HE MAKES IT IN TIME...
YES. POOR VIGFÚS. I HEARD HE'D LOST A SHEEP THIS WINTER, AND NOW HIS WIFE'S SICK. FATE IS AGAINST HIM. I'M NOT EVEN SURE THAT HE CAN AFFORD THE MEDICINE...
IT ONLY COST FIVE RIGSDALERS.
FIVE RIGSDALERS! WELL, MERCHANTS AREN'T KNOWN FOR THEIR CHARITY! WERE YOU EQUALLY CONSIDERATE WITH THE FRENCH?
DON'T MOCK ME, JÓN. TIMES ARE HARD FOR US ALL. THE FRENCH WERE SOAKING WET AND FROZEN STIFF, SO I JUST ACCEPTED THIS MEDALLION FOR TWO BLANKETS...
THAT BETTER?
IT'LL ONLY BE BETTER ONCE WE'RE BACK ON BOARD.
LET US DEPART THIS BARREN LAND. YOU KNOW WHAT THEY CALL SHRUBS HERE? TREES!
AND THE LAD?
HE WANTED TO LEAVE. IT'S HIS CHOICE, AND THE OPTIONS ARE FEW: HE'LL EITHER DIE OF COLD OR OF HUNGER.
WAAAH
WAAAH
WAAAH
WAAAH

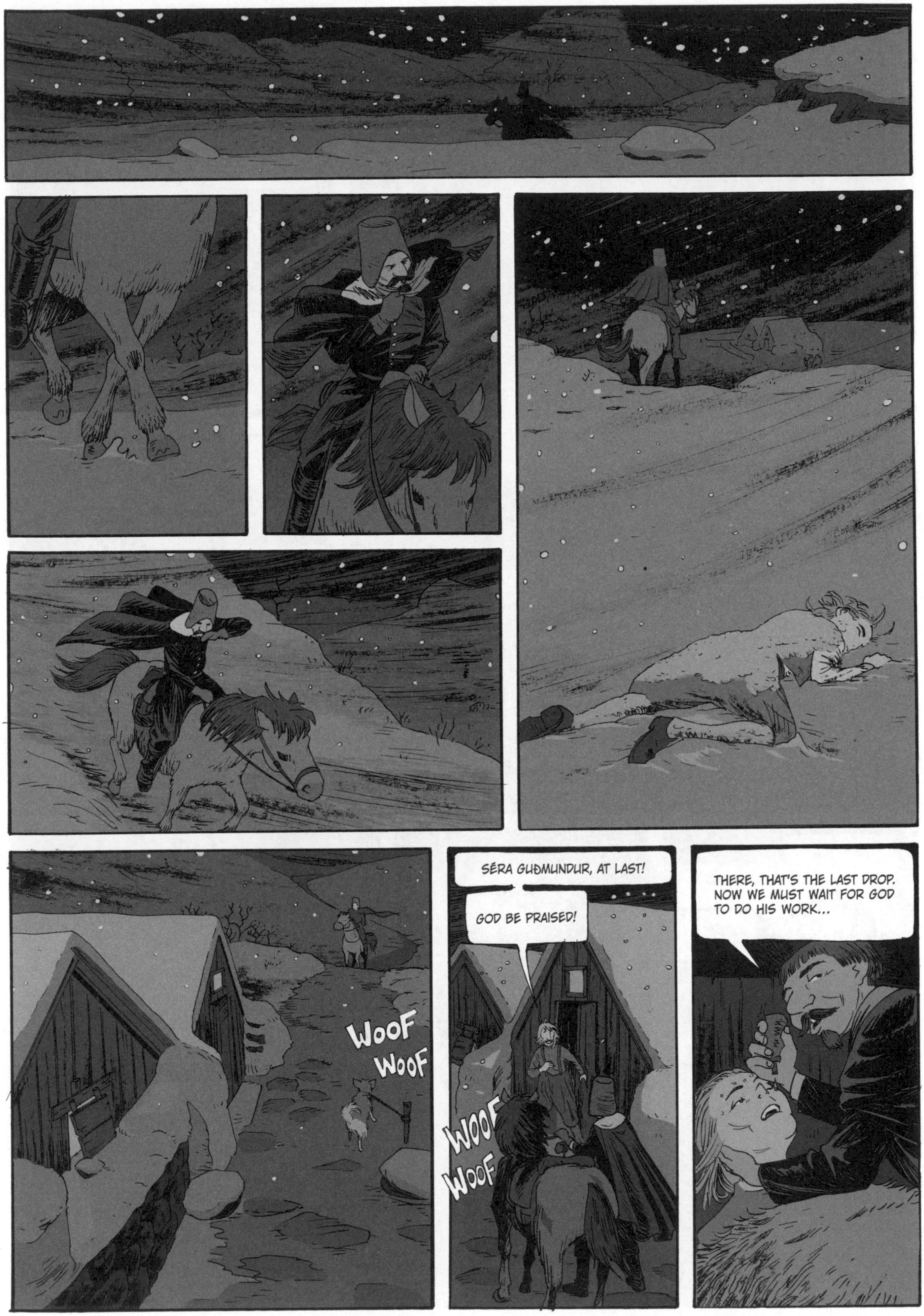
WOOF
WOOF
SÉRA GUÐMUNDUR, AT LAST!
GOD BE PRAISED!
WOOF
WOOF
THERE, THAT'S THE LAST DROP. NOW WE MUST WAIT FOR GOD TO DO HIS WORK...

THIS WINTER HAS BEEN HARSH, YOU KNOW. I LOST A SHEEP... WE'RE SHORT OF HAY... I CAN'T PAY RIGHT AWAY, BUT PLEASE SHARE OUR HUMBLE MEAL...
GLADLY.
I GRATEFULLY ACCEPT YOUR OFFER.
THEN, ACCEPT TO SHARE OUR BED, TOO. WE CAN'T LET YOU GO OUT IN SUCH A STORM.
WHAT DO YOU SAY TO SOME HOT BROTH?
THE HEAVENS WILL SHOW THEIR GRATITUDE, VIGFÚS. YOU ARE A GOOD MAN...
AND A POOR ONE...
IF THE LORD LOOKS AFTER THE NEEDY AS HIS OWN, HE'LL TAKE PITY ON ME.
YOUR WIFE WILL GET BETTER. I WILL PRAY FOR HER...
I HOPE SO, OR I'LL NEVER GET OVER IT.
HAVE FAITH!
HERE, STÍNA!
GO AND FETCH SOME SNOW. WE NEED IT TO BOIL THE—
WOOF WOOF
WHAT?!
WHAT THE DEVIL?!
DO NOT CURSE, MY SON!
WOOF WOOF
WERE YOU EXPECTING ANYONE?
NO...
JÓN?
I BRING DREADFUL TIDINGS...

NEVER SEEN HIM BEFORE. NO IDEA WHO HE IS. I FOUND HIM ON THE ROAD.
IF NOT FOR YOU, HIS ROAD WOULD BE ENDED.
WAIT, THAT'S NOT ALL. HE'S DOUBLY LUCKY – HE JUST AVOIDED A MASSACRE!
WHAT?
THE LORD TOOK HIM UNDER HIS WING...
A FOREIGN BOAT LANDED A COUPLE OF HOURS AGO...
YES...
IT WAS FRENCH, I BELIEVE?
I THINK THE BOY'S ONE OF THEM. THEY WERE LOOKING FOR HIM BEFORE THEY LEFT...
JUST AS THEY REACHED THEIR SHIP, A MUCH LARGER DANISH VESSEL SAILED UP THE FJORD...
IT MUST HAVE ENCOUNTERED THEM BEFORE; IT OPENED FIRE IMMEDIATELY... CAUGHT UNAWARES, THE FRENCH WERE POWERLESS... THE LANDING PARTY NARROWLY ESCAPED THAT FIRST ATTACK...
BUT THE DERANGED DANES CHASED THEM, SHOOTING INDISCRIMINATELY. THEY MUST HAVE REALISED THERE'D BEEN ILLEGAL TRADING AND METED OUT THEIR OWN JUSTICE...
BANG
BANG
BANG
WE WERE TERRIFIED AND TRIED TO FLEE. POOR MAGNÚS FELL BEHIND AND GOT SHOT IN THE BACK.
MY GOD! AND THEN?
I DIDN'T HANG AROUND, BUT I DOUBT THAT THOSE SKUNKS WERE SUBTLE ABOUT IT...
THEY THINK THEY OWN US!
I MUST LEAVE. WOULDN'T WANT TO DRAW THEM HERE.
WAIT... HAVE SOME BROTH WITH US FIRST.
THANKS, BUT QUICKLY.
WHAT ABOUT THE FRENCH LAD? I DON'T WANT HIM HERE.
WARM HIM UP FOR NOW. I'LL BE BACK FOR HIM LATER...
ANYWAY, HE MIGHT BE DEAD BY TOMORROW...

DON'T YOU WORRY. I'LL INFORM THE BAILIFF OF THIS CARNAGE. HE MUST HEAR HOW THE BASTARDS TREAT US. SADLY, I'M AFRAID THE LORD HIMSELF HAS ABANDONED US.
NEVER FEAR... THEY WILL PAY THE TOLL IN THE KINGDOM OF HEAVEN.
A NICER LIFE DOWN HERE WOULDN'T HURT IN THE MEANTIME!
RIGHT!
YOU'RE MISTAKEN... THE MEANING OF LIFE IS TO SAVE OUR SOULS.
INCIDENTALLY, MAY I HOPE TO SEE MORE OF YOU IN CHURCH THIS YEAR?
WHAT—?!
DON'T WORRY, IT'S ONLY VELLUM! I USE IT FOR STOCK, TO ADD FLAVOUR. I'M NOT ALL THAT RICH, YOU KNOW...
IT'S PARCHMENT... SOME PARTS ARE STILL READABLE.
LET ME SEE!
IT'S SKALDIC, ONE OF THE FINEST MEDIAEVAL POEMS: ABOUT THE DECLINE OF OUR PEOPLE, TOO BUSY SURVIVING TO FEED OUR SOULS...
SAVE OUR SOULS!
ARE THERE ANY MORE, DEAR VIGFÚS?
I THINK SO. LET ME SEE.
HERE'S ANOTHER... LOVELY LEATHER. MY MOTHER MADE IT INTO SHOES.
MAY I TAKE THESE IN PAYMENT FOR THE MEDICINE? THERE IS AN EMISSARY IN SKÁLHOLT WHO SEEKS OLD MANUSCRIPTS FOR HIS COLLECTION IN COPENHAGEN.
VERY WELL, IF YOU WISH.
IN DENMARK! THOSE DANES AGAIN...
THANK YOU, BUT I MUST BE OFF. GOOD NIGHT TO YOU.
RIDE SAFELY, JÓN.
ZZZ
ZZZ
I THOUGHT SO...
VIGFÚS DIDN'T SHOW ME ALL OF THEM...

HELLO, DAD. WHAT HAPPENED TO SÉRA GUÐMUNDUR?
HE LEFT FOR SKÁLHOLT VERY EARLY THIS MORNING, AS IF THE DEVIL WERE AFTER HIM. DON'T KNOW WHAT GOT INTO HIM.
I WANTED TO THANK HIM. MAMA'S FEELING MUCH BETTER NOW.
HE MANAGED TO BRING DOWN HER FEVER...
SHE'S EVEN ASKING FOR SOME FOOD.
THE LORD HAS SPARED US... LET'S MAKE HER A NICE BREAKFAST.
THE FRENCH LAD...
HOW'S HE DOING TODAY?
BAAAA
YAWN

WELL... HE LOOKS A LOT BETTER.
WHERE ARE YOU RUNNING OFF TO, EH?
THAT'S OUR SKIN YOU'RE WEARING... WHAT ARE YOU HIDING? SHOW ME!
DON'T SAY THAT! HE DOESN'T LOOK LIKE A THIEF.
RELAX. HE CAN'T UNDERSTAND. MIGHT BE A RUNT, BUT DON'T FORGET WHERE HE'S FROM. HE'S FRENCH! I DON'T TRUST THEM. YOU KNOW WHAT THEY SAY!
NO, I DON'T! BUT WE'VE NEVER SEEN ONE BEFORE...
HE'S THE SORT WHO'D HOODWINK US, I TELL YOU... AND HE'D BE NO USE ON THE FARM, EITHER. LOOK WHAT A WEAKLING...
SNIFF
SNIFF
DON'T JUDGE TOO SOON, DAD.
HERE, THIS IS FOR YOUR NOSE.
A REAL MILKSOP! HE WON'T BE ABLE TO SURVIVE UP HERE...
THAT'S VERY KIND OF YOU...
YOU SPEAK ICELANDIC!
?
INCREDIBLE! YOU SEE, HE IS GOOD AT SOMETHING!
DEVILRY, MORE LIKE...
COME ON... LET'S GO IN AND HAVE A TALK OVER SOME NICE, HOT MILK.

JACQUES!
WHAT ARE YOU DOING? YOU'RE STILL SICK... I WARN YOU...
IT ISN'T WISE!
I NEED AIR. I'M NOT USED TO THE SMELL. DO YOU ALWAYS LIVE WITH YOUR ANIMALS?
IT'S HOW WE KEEP WARM IN WINTER. THERE ISN'T MUCH FIREWOOD AROUND.
BUT THAT'S NOT WHY YOU'RE HERE, IS IT? DON'T BE SCARED OF DAD; HE WON'T BITE. WE SEE SO FEW FOREIGNERS. HE DIDN'T SHOW IT, BUT I KNOW HE WAS HAPPY YOU VOLUNTEERED TO WORK THROUGH THE WINTER WITH US HERE IN SNOTRUNES.
MY BROTHER'S ABROAD AND HE WON'T BE BACK FOR A FEW MONTHS... THERE WILL BE LOTS TO DO AT LAMBING TIME...
I'VE NEVER DONE IT!
YOU'LL CATCH ON. WITH YOUR SLENDER HANDS, IT'LL BE FINE.
I SAW THAT YOU WERE WRITING...
WHAT IS IT?
DRAWING, NOT WRITING. BUT I DON'T LIKE TO SHOW ANYONE. IT'S PRIVATE!
YOU'RE STRANGE!
I DON'T GET IT... I'M WONDERING HOW YOU LEARNED ICELANDIC SO WELL... IT'S A TOUGH LANGUAGE, WE'RE TOLD.
I KNOW – YOU AREN'T HUMAN! MAYBE YOU'RE AN ELF?!
THAT'S RUBBISH!
WELL ... I BELIEVE IN IT...
COME... I WANT TO SHOW YOU SOMETHING.
ONCE, A FOREIGN LADY MOVED HERE. SLOWLY SHE GAINED THE LOCALS' TRUST, TOOK CHARGE OF THE AREA, AND GREW WEALTHY. AT THE END OF EACH YEAR, SHE WOULD ISSUE A CHALLENGE: THE WINNER HAD TO SAY WHERE SHE WENT FROM CHRISTMAS TILL THE NEW YEAR. NO ONE COULD GUESS, AND CHALLENGERS DISAPPEARED ONE AFTER ANOTHER...
ATCHOO!

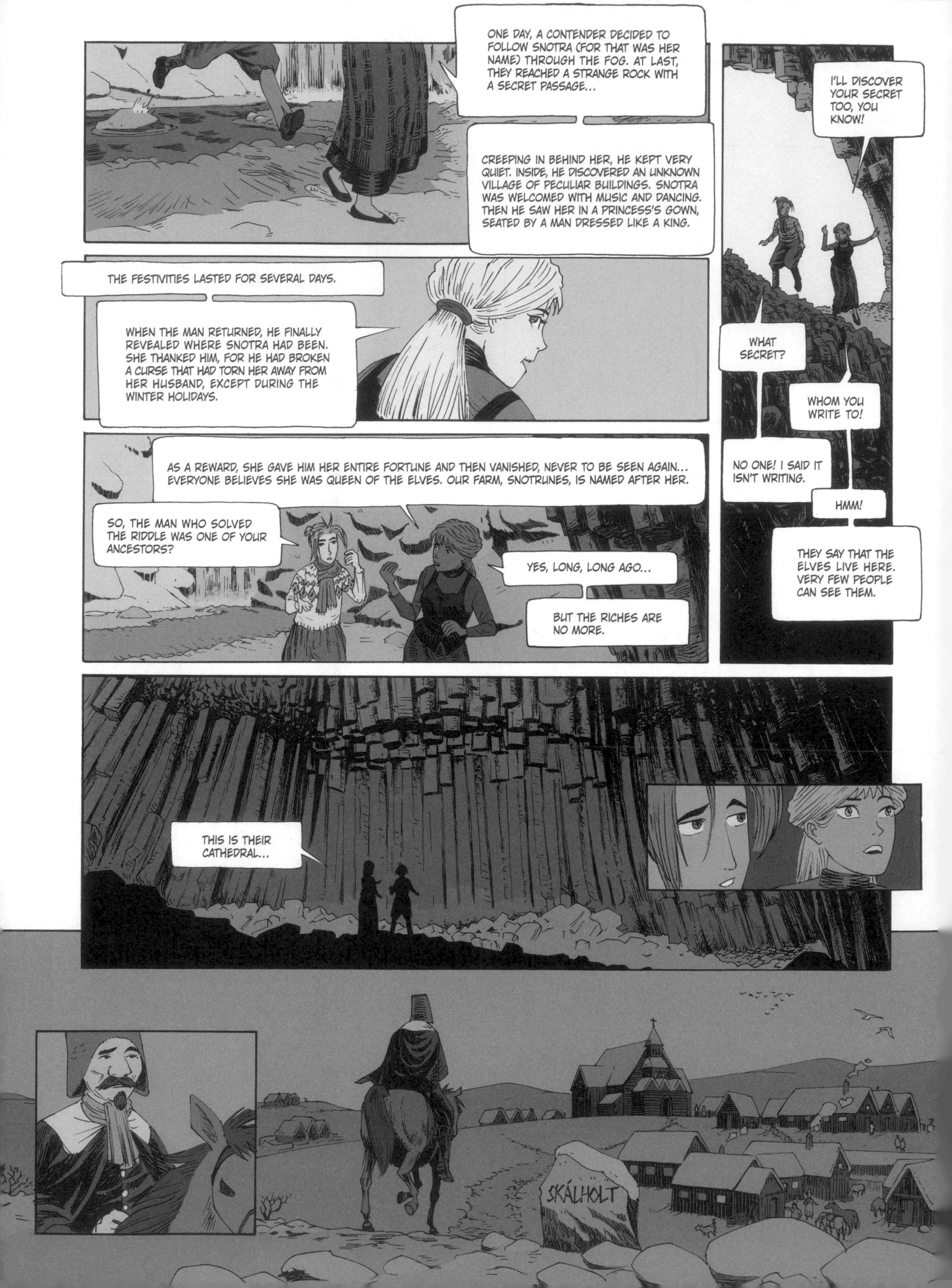
ONE DAY, A CONTENDER DECIDED TO FOLLOW SNOTRA (FOR THAT WAS HER NAME) THROUGH THE FOG. AT LAST, THEY REACHED A STRANGE ROCK WITH A SECRET PASSAGE...
CREEPING IN BEHIND HER, HE KEPT VERY QUIET. INSIDE, HE DISCOVERED AN UNKNOWN VILLAGE OF PECULIAR BUILDINGS. SNOTRA WAS WELCOMED WITH MUSIC AND DANCING. THEN HE SAW HER IN A PRINCESS'S GOWN, SEATED BY A MAN DRESSED LIKE A KING.
THE FESTIVITIES LASTED FOR SEVERAL DAYS.
WHEN THE MAN RETURNED, HE FINALLY REVEALED WHERE SNOTRA HAD BEEN. SHE THANKED HIM, FOR HE HAD BROKEN A CURSE THAT HAD TORN HER AWAY FROM HER HUSBAND, EXCEPT DURING THE WINTER HOLIDAYS.
AS A REWARD, SHE GAVE HIM HER ENTIRE FORTUNE AND THEN VANISHED, NEVER TO BE SEEN AGAIN... EVERYONE BELIEVES SHE WAS QUEEN OF THE ELVES. OUR FARM, SNOTRUNES, IS NAMED AFTER HER.
SO, THE MAN WHO SOLVED THE RIDDLE WAS ONE OF YOUR ANCESTORS?
YES, LONG, LONG AGO...
BUT THE RICHES ARE NO MORE.
I'LL DISCOVER YOUR SECRET TOO, YOU KNOW!
WHAT SECRET?
WHOM YOU WRITE TO!
NO ONE! I SAID IT ISN'T WRITING.
HMM!
THEY SAY THAT THE ELVES LIVE HERE. VERY FEW PEOPLE CAN SEE THEM.
THIS IS THEIR CATHEDRAL...
SKÁLHOLT

…EVERY DAY SHE TIGHTENED THE RIBBONS ROUND HER BELLY TO HIDE THAT SHE WAS WITH CHILD. AS GUNNA FELT THE DAY OF THE BIRTH DRAW NEARER, SHE COULD NO LONGER HIDE THE CHILD THAT BETRAYED HER ADULTEROUS UNION. IF HER SECRET WAS DISCOVERED, SHE KNEW SHE WOULD BE TAKEN TO ÞINGVELLIR* FOR TRIAL AND PROBABLY SENTENCED TO DROWNING IN THE ÖXARÁ RIVER.
WHEN THE FIRST CONTRACTIONS CAME, GUNNA RAN OFF INTO THE WILDS TO GIVE BIRTH ALONE, FAR FROM PRYING EYES…
PAINFUL THOUGH IT WAS, HER MIND WAS MADE UP. HER ONLY CHOICE WAS TO ABANDON HER NEWBORN IN THE HOPE THAT NATURE WOULD TAKE IT SWIFTLY, CUT SHORT ITS SUFFERING, AND QUICKLY SILENCE ITS CRIES.
GUNNA CONFESSED HER AWFUL SECRET BEFORE SHE DIED. TO THIS DAY, THE CHILD'S GHOST IS SAID TO HAUNT THE HRAUNDALUR VALLEY IN BORGARFJÖRÐUR. SOME SAY YOU CAN HEAR IT CRYING ON ITS BIRTHDAY EVERY YEAR: FEBRUARY 28.
TOMORROW I'LL READ YOU THE SAGA OF GRETTIR THE STRONG.
EVERYONE TO BED. WE HAVE TO MAKE OUR CANDLES LAST THROUGH THE WINTER.
LOOK AT YOUR FACE! WE LOVE TELLING GHOST STORIES HERE IN ICELAND.
IT'S JUST THAT … BEFORE I ENDED UP HERE…
DURING THE STORM LAST WEEK…
I WAS LOST IN THE MOUNTAINS. I THOUGHT I WAS GOING MAD, BUT I HEARD A BABY CRYING THROUGH THE WIND. I WAS AFRAID… WASN'T THAT ABOUT THE TIME OF THE BIRTHDAY?
YOU'RE TRYING TO SCARE ME!
BECAUSE I BELIEVE IT!
OH!
HAS SOMEONE TOUCHED MY THINGS? WAS IT YOU BY ANY CHANCE, FRENCHY?!
MY OLD BOOK OF MAGIC IS MISSING…
GENTLEMEN, WE ARE LOOKING AT CONFIRMATION OF THIS MAN'S HERESY.
YOU MAY TAKE THE OTHER PARCHMENTS FOR YOUR COLLECTION, MY DEAR ÁRNI, BUT ALLOW ME TO KEEP THIS ONE AS EVIDENCE.
AS YOU WISH, MY LORD.
VIGFÚS MUST QUICKLY PROVE THAT HE HAS NOT ENGAGED IN SORCERY OR BE BURNED AT THE STAKE.
YOU ARE RIGHT.
SUCH PRACTICES CANNOT BE ACCEPTED IN YOUR DIOCESE, MY LORD.

*THE OUTDOOR MEETING PLACE WHERE THE COUNTRY'S HIGH DIGNITARIES WOULD GATHER EACH JUNE FOR THE *ALÞINGI* (PARLIAMENTARY ASSEMBLY AND COURT)

GOSH! THE WATER REALLY IS HOT!
WANT TO TRY IT? IT'D BE GOOD FOR YOUR BRONCHITIS! WE OFTEN BATHE HERE.
EVEN IN WINTER?
IT'S EVEN BETTER!
I'M TEMPTED...
SO, GO ON!
ALL RIGHT, YOU CAN PUT THE CLOTH DOWN THERE.
FINE, I'M GOING... YOU THINK I WANT TO SEE YOU NAKED?!
VIGFÚS VIGFÚÚS
VIGFÚÚS VIGFÚÚÚS
VIGFÚÚS
I'M OVER HERE!
WHY ON EARTH ARE YOU YELLING LIKE THAT?
OUT WITHOUT A HAT? NOT WISE IN YOUR CONDITION!
THE TRAP WORKED. HERE'S OUR DINNER FOR TONIGHT.
BUT, WHAT WAS IT THAT YOU WANTED?
COME AND SEE... A SHEEP IS—
WHAT ARE YOU TALKING ABOUT?
WHAT'S THIS DEVILRY?!

I CALL ON LORD GOD, ÓÐINN THE CREATOR, THOR, FREYR, AND JESUS CHRIST TO PROTECT US AND OUR ANIMALS IN OUR HUMBLE ABODE.
I CARVE THIS MAGICAL ÆGISHJÁLMUR SIGIL TO OUST THE DEMON AND EVIL LOKI.
WHAT ARE YOU MAKING, DAD?
A PROTECTIVE TOTEM?
I PROBABLY FORGOT SOME OF THE LATIN WORDS. I LOST MY BOOK OF MAGIC...
LET'S JUST HOPE IT'LL DO.
OUR FARM'S HAUNTED BY AN EVIL SPIRIT!

TRY TO GRAB ITS LEGS!
THAT'S RIGHT! GO ON, PULL!
PULL!
AGAIN! THAT'S IT! HERE IT COMES!
I DID IT! I DID IT!
YOUR FIRST LAMBING.
NOW GIVE IT TO ITS MOTHER, AND SHE'LL LICK IT TILL IT'S CLEAN.
BAAA
YOU'D MAKE A GOOD FARMER...
BLOOD!
YOUR HANDKERCHIEF IS ALL BLOODY!
WE'LL HAVE TO GET THE PASTOR BACK TO HEAL YOU. I'M WORRIED!
GET RID OF THAT FRENCHY AND WE'LL ALL BE FINE AGAIN!
YOU CAN'T BLAME HIM FOR YOUR RELAPSE AND THE DEAD SHEEP!
BUT I CAN SENSE IT!
MADNESS! THE FEVER'S MAKING YOU DELIRIOUS! I'M GETTING TO KNOW HIM! LOOK HOW USEFUL HE WAS DURING THE LAMBING, AND NOW HE'S OFF HUNTING WITH DAD. HE'S BEEN A GREAT HELP WHILE EGILL'S AWAY.
IT'S SO HIGH! AT LEAST I'M NOT AFRAID OF HEIGHTS. I GOT USED TO ALL THAT...
...ON THE SHIP!
HEY!
SHTACK

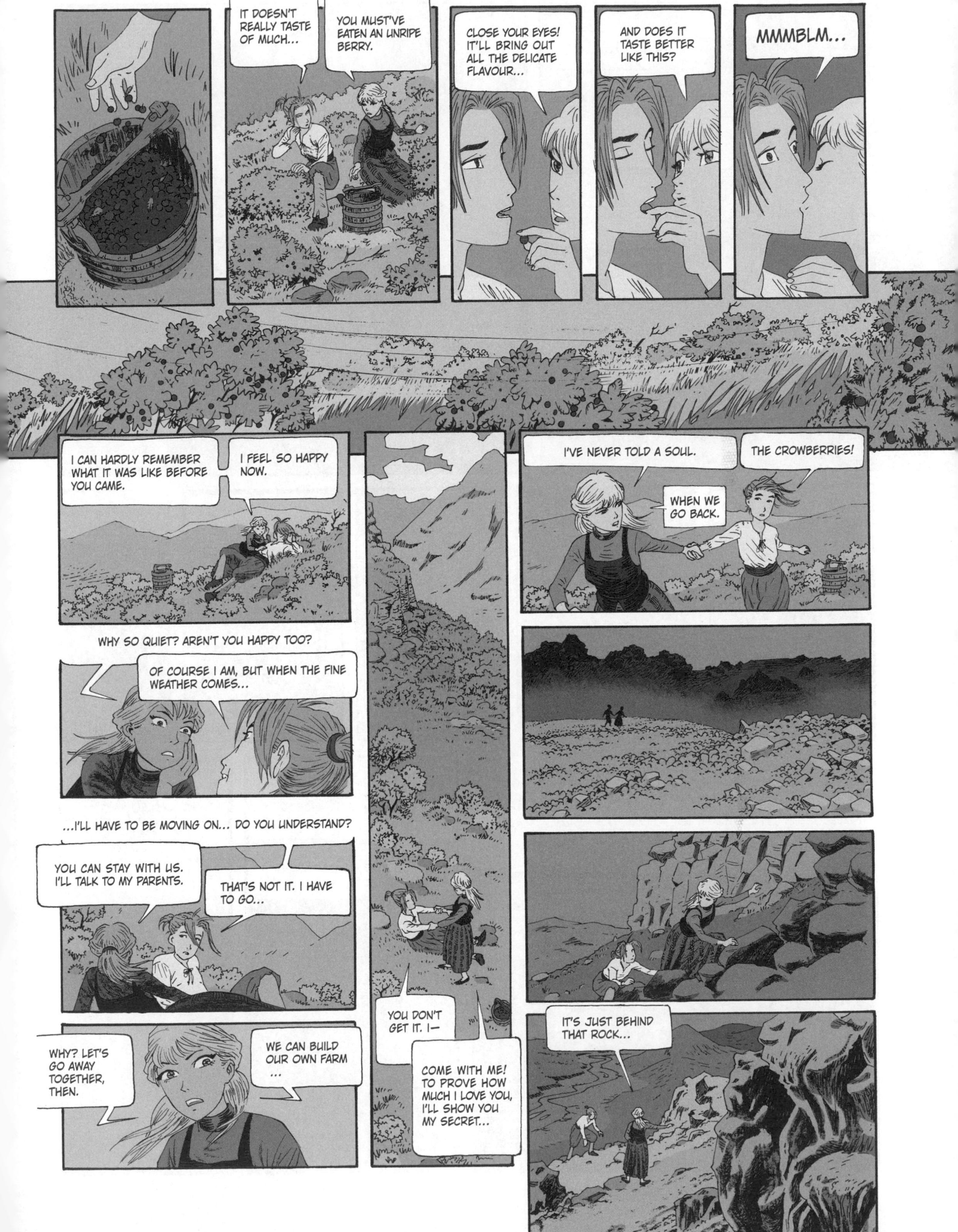
IT DOESN'T REALLY TASTE OF MUCH...
YOU MUST'VE EATEN AN UNRIPE BERRY.
CLOSE YOUR EYES! IT'LL BRING OUT ALL THE DELICATE FLAVOUR...
AND DOES IT TASTE BETTER LIKE THIS?
MMMBLM...
I CAN HARDLY REMEMBER WHAT IT WAS LIKE BEFORE YOU CAME.
I FEEL SO HAPPY NOW.
WHY SO QUIET? AREN'T YOU HAPPY TOO?
OF COURSE I AM, BUT WHEN THE FINE WEATHER COMES...
...I'LL HAVE TO BE MOVING ON... DO YOU UNDERSTAND?
YOU CAN STAY WITH US. I'LL TALK TO MY PARENTS.
THAT'S NOT IT. I HAVE TO GO...
WHY? LET'S GO AWAY TOGETHER, THEN.
WE CAN BUILD OUR OWN FARM ...
YOU DON'T GET IT. I—
COME WITH ME! TO PROVE HOW MUCH I LOVE YOU, I'LL SHOW YOU MY SECRET...
I'VE NEVER TOLD A SOUL.
THE CROWBERRIES!
WHEN WE GO BACK.
IT'S JUST BEHIND THAT ROCK...

IT'S ONLY A TREE!
ISN'T IT AMAZING?
IT'S THE BIGGEST TREE I'VE EVER SEEN!
WELL, YOU KNOW, IN FRANCE...
HEY! WATCH OUT! DON'T FALL!
THIS IS MY TREE. I'M SAFE HERE.
...
THAT'S NOT FUNNY! GIVE ME BACK MY BOOK!
COME AND GET IT!
OH MY, YOU'RE A REAL ARTIST!
YOU NEVER TOLD ME.
BUT THIS... I RECOGNISE THESE... THEY'RE...
...MAGICAL SYMBOLS!
ARE YOU A SORCERER?
NO, NO! I DON'T KNOW WHAT THEY MEAN. THOSE SYMBOLS HAVE BEEN IN MY HEAD SINCE I WAS LITTLE, HAUNTING ME AT NIGHT, SO I TRY TO DRAW THEM. I SEE LANDSCAPES, TOO. ONE DAY, WHILE LEAFING THROUGH A TRAVEL JOURNAL, I REALISED IT WAS ICELAND. THE ENGRAVINGS WERE JUST LIKE MY DREAMS, SO I STUCK THEM IN HERE.
WHAT?! ALL THAT FUSS OVER PICTURES THAT YOU DIDN'T EVEN DRAW?!
SOME ARE MINE... SEE THESE ROCKS? I'VE DREAMED OF THEM SO OFTEN THAT I MANAGED TO DRAW THEM.
DO YOU HAVE ANY IDEA WHERE THEY MIGHT BE?
THE WHOLE COUNTRY IS COVERED IN LAVA. IF IT'S A SPECIAL PLACE, PERHAPS YOU COULD FIND SOMETHING IN THE SKÁLHOLT ARCHIVES.

BUT, FORGET ABOUT IT, JACQUES! DO YOU REALLY MEAN TO LEAVE US JUST TO FIND THOSE ROCKS? YOU SHOULD KEEP AS FAR AWAY FROM THEM AS YOU CAN. STAY HERE...
...WITH ME.
YOU DON'T UNDERSTAND! THESE VISIONS HAVE OBSESSED ME FOR YEARS. I'M SURE THAT'S WHERE THE ANSWER LIES.
IT SOUNDS LIKE YOU NEED A PASTOR... IF YOU AREN'T A SORCERER, BURN YOUR BOOK. IT'S USELESS!
FORGET IT! OUR HAPPINESS IS WHAT MATTERS.
I NEED TO KNOW. THERE'S MORE: THE OTHER DAY, WHEN YOUR FATHER CAME BACK FROM THE HUNT WITH A BROKEN JAW, HE DIDN'T FALL LIKE HE SAID... I DON'T KNOW WHY, BUT HE ATTACKED ME, AND I DEFENDED MYSELF. THEN HE FORGOT ALL ABOUT IT. I DON'T UNDERSTAND...
AND IT HAPPENED TO ME BEFORE: ON THE SHIP, I NEARLY GOT STABBED FOR NO REASON AT ALL!
......
AND WHEN YOU FIND THE ANSWER, WILL YOU COME BACK?
I WILL.
OH! I THINK I UNDERSTAND. THAT MIGHT EXPLAIN IT...
WHAT MIGHT?
IT'S AS IF AN EVIL SPIRIT IS AFTER YOU, HAUNTING YOU...
MY MOTHER SENSED SOMETHING...
I'M SCARED OF YOU NOW, JACQUES...
WAAAH!
STOP IT! THAT'S NOT FUNNY!
COME ON, I'M SORRY! I WAS ONLY BEING SILLY!
IT'S JUST A LOAD OF OLD SUPERSTITIONS.

YOU MADE ME TELL THAT STORY... I KNEW THAT I SHOULDN'T HAVE...
HEY!
WHAT IS IT?
I THINK MY BROTHER'S BACK...
YES, IT'S HIM! I CAN TELL.
EGILL!
BUT, WHAT'S WRONG?
IT'S MOTHER... I CAME BACK TOO LATE. SHE'S—

SCRATCHSCRATCH
SCRATCH
MAYBE THE FOX FRIGHTENED THE SHEEP AND ONE OF THEM PANICKED, JUMPED, GOT CAUGHT UP IN A ROPE, AND HANGED ITSELF BY ACCIDENT? THERE'S NOTHING SUPERNATURAL TO IT! I'M NOT RESPONSIBLE FOR ALL YOUR WOES, AS YOU SAY...
COME AND SEE WHAT I'VE FOUND! THERE'S A HOLE IN THE WALL AND A FOX SQUEEZED OUT.
I DON'T CARE. STÍNA TOLD US EVERYTHING. WE WANT NO MORE OF YOU HERE. BEGONE!
AND DON'T YOU DARE COME BACK, OR I'LL DEAL WITH YOU PERSONALLY!
I'M SORRY, JACQUES, BUT MY MOTHER'S DEATH HAS—
DON'T WORRY, IT WAS TIME THAT I LEFT... IF ONLY IT COULD'VE BEEN UNDER NICER CIRCUMSTANCES...
BAAA
I CAN'T JUST LET YOU GO LIKE THAT... WAIT FOR ME IN MY SECRET PLACE AND I'LL JOIN YOU IN AN HOUR. I'LL BRING SOME DRIED FISH FOR YOUR JOURNEY.

FATHER!
WE HAVE COMPANY!
IT MUST BE GUÐMUNDUR. NO, WAIT... IT LOOKS MORE LIKE THE BAILIFF...
SUCH A RARE VISITOR! MY WIFE WOULD'VE BEEN PROUD TO SEE YOU HERE IN ALL YOUR FINERY...
...BUT, SADLY, IT'S A PASTOR'S BLESSING WE NEED.
I'M SORRY ABOUT YOUR WIFE, BUT THAT ISN'T WHY I CAME... BISHOP BRYNJÒLFUR SENDS ME.
HE SUSPECTS YOU OF PRACTISING SORCERY. YOU WILL BE TRIED AT THE ALPINGI.
YOU CAN'T DO THIS TO ME... I'VE ALWAYS BEEN AN HONEST WORKER!
SÉRA GUÐMUNDUR VISITED YOUR HOUSE AND FOUND A BOOK OF SPELLS THERE.
BUT THAT PROVES **NOTHING!**
YOU KNOW THAT, SINCE THE REFORMATION, OWNING SUCH OBJECTS IS PUNISHABLE BY LAW.
AND WHAT IS **THAT?**
COME ALONG NOW, WITHOUT A FUSS!

STÍNA! IS IT YOU?
I SEE YOU'RE EMPTY-HANDED… NEVER MIND; DON'T LOOK SO SAD. I'LL MAKE DO ALONG THE WAY. I'M USED TO IT.
WHY DID YOU DO IT?!
WHAT?
DAMN YOU! IS THIS HOW YOU THANK US, BY TAKING REVENGE ON MY FATHER?!
WHAT INSANITY IS THIS NOW?! IT'S YOUR FATHER WHO'S NEVER LIKED ME…
WHAT'LL BECOME OF US AND THE FARM WITHOUT HIM? THE BAILIFF ARRESTED HIM. HE FACES DEATH!
BUT … IT WASN'T ME!
REALLY? I'M STARTING TO THINK YOU CAST A SPELL ON US. WE NEVER HAD SO MUCH BAD LUCK BEFORE YOU CAME!
I DON'T BELIEVE YOU. YOU'RE FINISHED! LOOK WHO'S WITH ME…
YOU TOO, STÍNA? YOU'RE…
WAIT, EGILL! THINK ABOUT IT!

THIS IS LUNACY! YOU CAN'T BLAME EVERYTHING ON ME...
WE'LL DISCUSS THAT LATER, BUT FIRST I'M GOING TO DEAL WITH YOU!
VERY WELL! YOU ASKED FOR IT! JUST IMAGINE IF IT'S TRUE...
THAT MEANS I HAVE THE POWER TO TAKE MY REVENGE ON YOU BOTH, HERE AND NOW!
BE CAREFUL, OR I'LL CURSE YOU FOR SEVERAL GENERATIONS!
KERRASH
KABOOMM

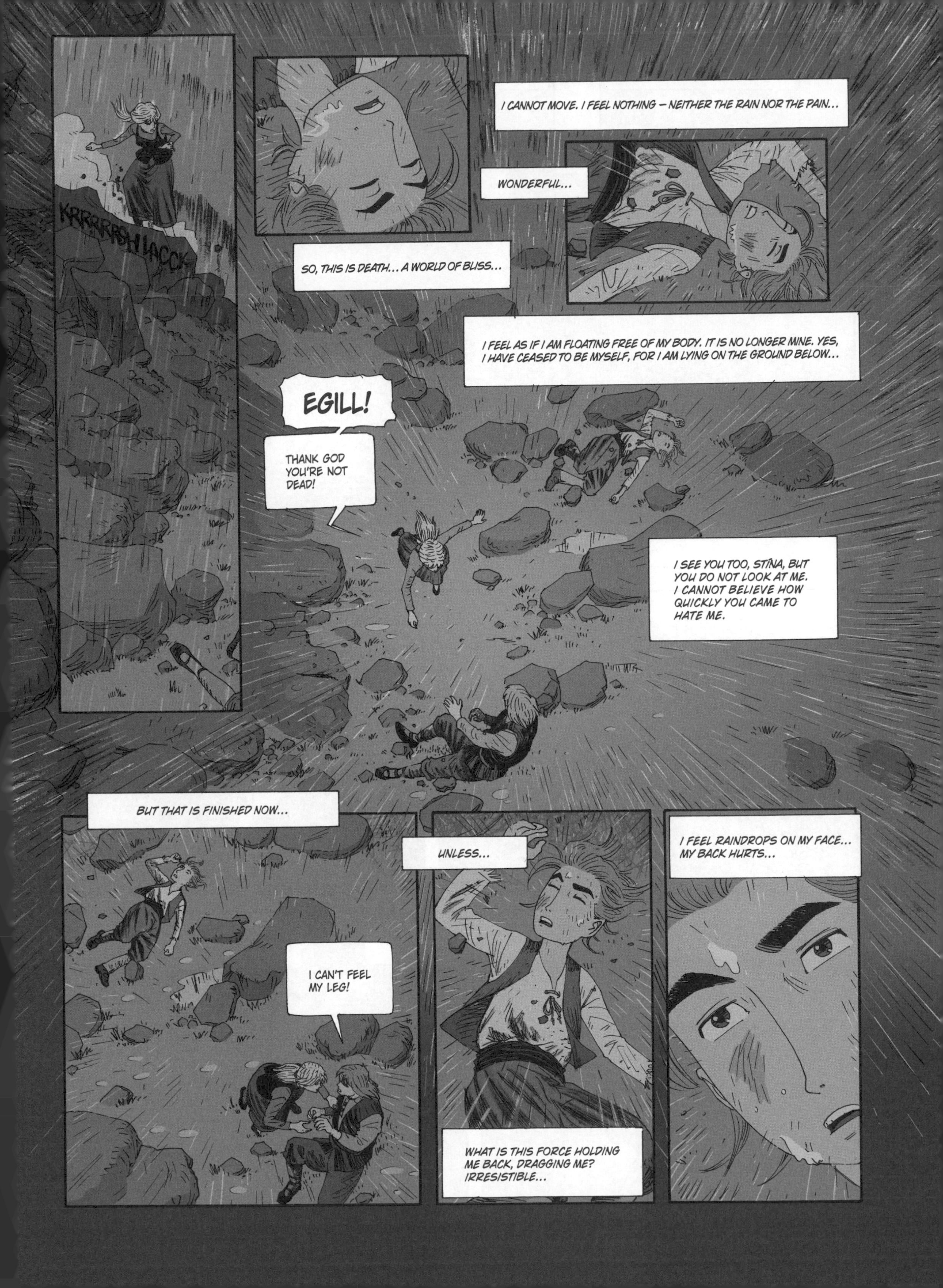
KRRRRRSH LACCK
I CANNOT MOVE. I FEEL NOTHING – NEITHER THE RAIN NOR THE PAIN…
WONDERFUL…
SO, THIS IS DEATH… A WORLD OF BLISS…
I FEEL AS IF I AM FLOATING FREE OF MY BODY. IT IS NO LONGER MINE. YES, I HAVE CEASED TO BE MYSELF, FOR I AM LYING ON THE GROUND BELOW…
EGILL!
THANK GOD YOU'RE NOT DEAD!
I SEE YOU TOO, STÍNA, BUT YOU DO NOT LOOK AT ME. I CANNOT BELIEVE HOW QUICKLY YOU CAME TO HATE ME.
BUT THAT IS FINISHED NOW…
I CAN'T FEEL MY LEG!
UNLESS…
WHAT IS THIS FORCE HOLDING ME BACK, DRAGGING ME? IRRESISTIBLE…
I FEEL RAINDROPS ON MY FACE… MY BACK HURTS…

YOU'LL BE ALL RIGHT. DON'T MOVE; I'LL MAKE A SPLINT.
HAS THAT FRENCH DEVIL BREATHED HIS LAST?
DON'T WORRY, HE'S—
HE WAS THERE!
I THOUGHT HE WAS DEAD!
BESSASTAÐIR – THE GOVERNOR'S RESIDENCE. THEREIN LIES YOUR FATE.
.....
WHAT HAVE WE DONE TO MAKE GOD TURN AGAINST US?
WERE WE VISITED BY SOME KIND OF DEMON?
I DON'T KNOW WHAT HE WAS...
...BUT IF I EVER FIND HIM, I WON'T MISS. THAT I PROMISE YOU!
I KNOW WHERE HE'S GOING...
TO SKÁLHOLT. HE WANTED TO LOOK IN THE ARCHIVES.

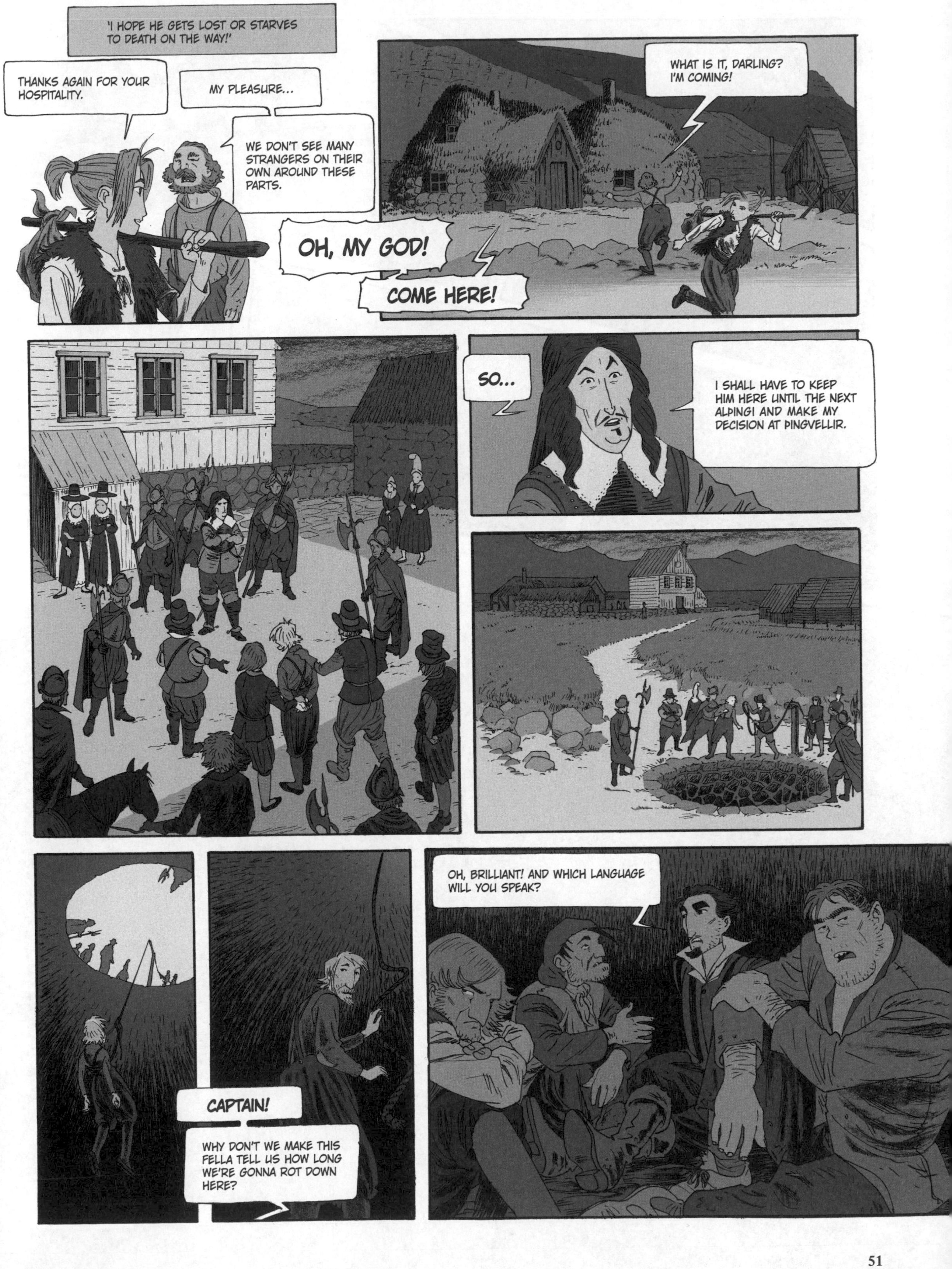
'I HOPE HE GETS LOST OR STARVES TO DEATH ON THE WAY!'
THANKS AGAIN FOR YOUR HOSPITALITY.
MY PLEASURE...
WE DON'T SEE MANY STRANGERS ON THEIR OWN AROUND THESE PARTS.
WHAT IS IT, DARLING? I'M COMING!
OH, MY GOD!
COME HERE!
SO...
I SHALL HAVE TO KEEP HIM HERE UNTIL THE NEXT ALPINGI AND MAKE MY DECISION AT PINGVELLIR.
CAPTAIN!
WHY DON'T WE MAKE THIS FELLA TELL US HOW LONG WE'RE GONNA ROT DOWN HERE?
OH, BRILLIANT! AND WHICH LANGUAGE WILL YOU SPEAK?

SKÁLHOLT!
AT LAST!
TO BE CONTINUED...